True G[

REAL DEMONIC POSSESSIONS AND EXORCISMS

BY ZACHERY KNOWLES

Real Demonic Possessions and Exorcisms
Copyright © 2017 by Zachery Knowles.

All rights reserved. No part of this book may be reproduced in any form without permission in writing from the author. Reviewers may quote brief passages in reviews

Published by **True Ghost Stories**

ISBN: 1544786549

ISBN-13: 978-1544786544

Disclaimer

No part of this publication may be reproduced or transmitted in any form or by any means, mechanical or electronic, including photocopying or recording, or by any information storage and retrieval system, or transmitted by email without permission in writing from the publisher.

While all attempts have been made to verify the information provided in this publication, neither the author nor the publisher assumes any responsibility for errors, omissions, or contrary interpretations of the subject matter herein.

This book is for entertainment purposes only. The views expressed are those of the author alone, and should not be taken as expert instruction or commands. The reader is responsible for his or her own actions.

Adherence to all applicable laws and regulations, including international, federal, state, and local governing professional licensing, business practices, advertising, and all other aspects of doing business in the US, Canada, or any other jurisdiction is the sole responsibility of the purchaser or reader.

Neither the author nor the publisher assumes any responsibility or liability whatsoever on the behalf of the purchaser or reader of these materials.

Any perceived slight of any individual or organization is purely unintentional.

YOUR FREE GIFT

As a way of saying thanks for your purchase, I'm offering a free eBook to readers of my *True Ghost Stories* series.

To instantly download the PDF version of my book, *Real Black-Eyed Kids*, all you need to do is visit:

<u>**www.realhorror.net**</u>

CONTENTS

INTRODUCTION..7
CLARITA VILLENEUVA: VAMPIRE GIRL..11
PRISCILLA JOHNSON: TERROR IN COLONIAL AMERICA.........17
JULIA: SATAN'S PRIESTESS 26
MICHAEL TAYLOR: FROM EXORCISM TO MURDER...................33
MASS POSSESSION AT THE ELSA PEREA FLORE SCHOOL........40
DAVID: THE BEAST MAN AND THE BOY......................................44
CHEYENNE: THE BEAST MAN AND THE NICE GUY 49
ANNA: MOST UNNATURAL 54
BILL RAMSEY: A REAL WEREWOLF? 62
CLARA GERMANA CELE: SNAKE GIRL 71
THIEBAULD & JOSEPH: THE POSSESSED BROTHERS................78
BEWITCHED SOPHIA 85
GISELLE: THE HOUSEWIFE AND THE HEALER 92
SLEEP WELL...100

INTRODUCTION

What you are about to read is a collection of stories—true stories—about demon possession. The individuals in these stories come from all walks of life, various time periods, and several different countries. The details of their stories may differ greatly, but there are certain things they all have in common: loss of control, torment, and fear. In fact, fear is rampant in these stories: personal fear, fear of insanity, fear of the stigma of demon possession, fear of some diabolical creature only they can see, fear for their loved ones safety, and fear for their very soul.

Keep in mind, with demon possession nothing is as it seems. Consider the Italian exorcist who had a frail, elderly woman brought to him for exorcism. At first, she seemed like a sweet, grandmotherly-type woman more likely to be carrying a fresh-baked pie rather than having a demon cast out of her. When alone in the room with the elderly woman, the exorcist turned his back to put on his stole; when he turned back to her, the tiny, frail, little old lady rose from the wooden chair in which she sat and held it over her head by one leg, growling out blasphemies with her face twisted beyond recognition.

Demon possession doesn't always manifest itself as shown in the movies, either. For instance, take the case of a rather chubby twelve-year old boy, Tim, who showed few signs of demon possession. What attracted the attention of people wasn't so much what he did, but the effect he had on others: just Tim's presence could cause a roomful of people to become angry and violent.

Many people are familiar with the infamous "pea soup" scene from *The Exorcist*, or a similar scene found in one of the old episodes of the *X-Files*. Believe it or not, it is not uncommon for individuals to vomit up strange substances during an exorcism, although projectile vomiting, as in the films, is more myth than truth. However, it is factual for people to vomit up far more than their physical body can hold including hair, teeth, nails, pins, feces, scarves, and even an occasional frog.

Another film favorite is strange voices and bestial sounds originating from the possessed. In this case, the truth is far more disturbing than fiction; the electronically-manipulated sounds in films do not hold a candle to the eerie, disturbing, unearthly sounds associated with real-life demon possession. As one nun put it, it often sounds like a choir of hellish animals, echoing from deep within the bowels of Hell, with Satan as their director. The voices heard are simply inhuman and to hear one in person will likely disturb you for the rest of your life.

Finally, there are some very dramatic exorcisms in this book that combine levitation, inhuman voices, clairvoyant knowledge, and much more. However, not all exorcisms are dramatic; case-in-point the story of Irish Presbyterian missionary Amy Carmichael. While serving in Japan, she noticed one of her neighbors had been possessed by several fox demons. The local Japanese exorcists had been working on the man for hours, but to no avail. Amy, and her translator Misaki-San, joined together in private prayer for several hours before visiting the man and his family. With his wife's permission, the two young women went in the room where he was restrained for the man's wife said Amy and Misaki-San couldn't hurt him anymore.

Securely restrained by several ropes, the man lie face-down on the floor with burn marks all over his back where the local exorcists had been burning incense to drive the demons away. His body was covered in sweat and every muscle was tense as he growled at the women. Amy and Misaki-San, both in their mid-twenties, stood before him and prayed a quiet, simple prayer of deliverance in the name of Jesus. As they turned to leave, Amy told the wife her husband would be fine. The next morning the women received word the man was once again well and wished to personally thank them for their prayers.

The villains in these stories are the demons that took possession of these individuals. While some of the possessed were promised advantages for cooperating with these dark powers, the horror they reaped in return outweighed any good that may have come. Physical pain, mental torment, a shortened life-span, separation from society, murderous urges, suicidal thoughts, and much, much more are among the house warming gifts demons transport when they take up residence in a human body.

In his book *An Exorcist Tells His Story*, Father Gabriele Amorth shares the experience of a young man who was demon possessed. This young, 16-year old man experienced deep depression, hopelessness, physical weakness, and a blackening of his soul. He described a sense of an unseen knife stabbing him, its goal not just to physically kill him, but to destroy him from the soul outward as well. He felt engulfed in darkness and completely helpless, his life circumducting out of control until he was finally delivered.

These stories are not only represented by villainous figures for there are heroes, too. Symbols such as a loved one refusing to give up on seeking help, a minister or priest who faces physical danger to emancipate the possessed, or teams of assistants who place their own physical and mental well-being at risk during exorcisms. Each of these heroes faced the demons knowing these spirits may reveal secret sins from their past, cause physical harm outside of the exorcism, and/or force them to see and hear things they would be hard pressed to forget.

Are you prepared to read some true stories about demon possession?

CLARITA VILLENEUVA: VAMPIRE GIRL

Clarita Villanueva was a petite, attractive teenage girl living a very rough life in the Philippines during the 1950s.

She was no stranger to the paranormal as she grew up watching her single mother hold séances and practice fortune-telling as a means to make money. However, when Clarita came face-to-face with the demonic, she was as helpless as the next person.

THE DEMONIC MANIFESTS

When her mother died, Clarita was left alone to fend for herself at the tender age of 12. She began as a vagabond, but was quickly lured into prostitution. She became quite skilled at plying her trade and focused on the capital city of Manila for maximum profit.

Late one night in 1953, when she was 18-year old, the Manila police arrested her on vagrancy and prostitution charges. It was at this time as she was locked up in a Bilibid prison cell that authorities discovered something was quite wrong with this young woman.

Clarita claimed two creatures had repeatedly attacked her over a period of nine days. Attributing this claim to mental illness, the officials paid little attention until bite marks began to appear on the her, most prominently on her neck, hence the nickname "vampire girl."

Soon Clarita was in the mayor's office accompanied by the chief medical examiner and a few other witnesses from various professions. There she began to writhe, laugh, and cry out as if experiencing pain; the group of witnesses observed bite marks appear where no bite marks had been. They stated the bite marks would appear under the palm of someone's hand as they held her arm, becoming visible once the hand was removed.

At one point, those present saw her make a motion as if pulling hair from someone or something invisible and then discovered a wad of thick, straight, black hair in her clenched fist. The hair clearly matched the description of her tormentors.

DESCRIPTION AND BEHAVIOR OF THE CREATURES

Clarita had described one of her attackers as a large man covered in thick, curly hair over his head, chest, and arms. He also had abnormally large teeth, much like that of a dog, and his eyes were sharp and piercing. The other creature was very short, just over two-feet tall, dressed in a black hooded robe with sharp, vampire teeth and bulging eyes.

The beings took turns biting her, Clarita claimed. The smaller one would climb around on her body to access new places to bite. They both preferred the fleshy areas of the body where it would be difficult for her to personally inflict a bite wound, favoring her upper torso, arms, and neck. Their bites would leave purplish, discolored bruises and sometimes moisture.

NEWSPAPER COVERAGE AND EXPERTS

As these horrific attacks continued, her story quickly attracted the attention of the media, making front-page news in the Philippines, the United States, and eventually all over the world. The news depicted her in a photo in which the attractive, dark-haired young girl's face and mouth were contorted in anguish while her eyes filled with desperation. One can only imagine the fear and helplessness Clarita felt; so young and with no family to care for her.

Another grainy newspaper photo reflects a beautiful young woman with her mouth stretched wide open in pain, eyes tightly shut, and reportedly in the throes of a seizure. Clarita began to fall into trances; subsequently seizures began to occur more frequently. During her trances, medical professionals, with over 100 called in during her experiences, tried pricking her skin with needles, but she had no reaction; it seemed as if her body was there, but Clarita was not.

Some of the medical experts, as to be expected, insisted her experiences were nothing more than manifestations of mental hysteria. They even insisted the bite marks were discolorations in the skin caused by her mind, yet they could not provide an explanation of how her mind could cause such marks.

Others who witnessed the same incidents disagreed with the medical professionals, affirming something invisible to all except Clarita was attacking her and they were all helpless to protect her. They also pointed to the saliva-like moisture that appeared around the bite marks as further refutation of this tenuous theory.

THE DEADLY CURSES

It is also worthy to note one outspoken skeptic who accused Clarita of putting on an act to garner attention was "cursed" by Clarita; according to onlookers, her normally large, expressive eyes narrowed and took on an almost snake-like appearance as she simply said to her skeptic, "You will die." Though it cannot be proven if she did curse him, the man died the next day.

He was not the only victim of such a "curse" by Clarita. One of the chief jailers had aggressively kicked Clarita for some perceived wrong-doing. In response, witnesses say she turned to face the guard and murmured the same words; within four days, the jailer, too, died.

Fear struck many in Manila as they came to believe Clarita was no mere victim of demonic torment but rather a powerful witch. The fact that her mother was a fortune-teller did not help matters.

PLEA FOR HELP

While many countries across the world offered ideas for cures and treatments, it seemed no Christian nation was brave enough to respond. After weeks of torment, help came to tortured Clarita in the form of an American minister, Lester Sumrall, working to help build-up some local Philippine churches. Lester Sumrall felt God brought him to help the girl and bravely approached the mayor and his team for permission to visit Clarita, stating she had a case of demonic possession.

Sumrall was a Protestant minister and thus did not perform a Roman Catholic exorcism, but he performed an exorcism all the same. As he began to confront the demons in the name of Jesus Christ, they began to speak through Clarita in two distinct voices, corresponding to the two demons Clarita professed to have witnessed. After a matter of days, Sumrall was confident Clarita was freed from their power until they returned and Sumrall once again confronted them in the name of Jesus. He finally cast them out for good and Clarita was encouraged to seek salvation to prevent further demonic possession.

Clarita was freed from her demons for the remainder of her days. She remained active in the church in the Philippines and went on to marry and have a family.

PRISCILLA JOHNSON: TERROR IN COLONIAL AMERICA

Priscilla Johnson was a teenage girl living in 1670s colonial America. A lean, intense, outgoing blonde sixteen-year old, she was working for the household of the local pastor to bring in some extra income for her family. However, it would seem the devil was waiting for her right outside the minister's home.

HORROR BEGINS

Her nightmare began with odd behavior observed by the pastor's family not long after Priscilla started working for them. They claimed she exhibited sudden changes in facial expressions, speaking to someone that simply wasn't there, and unreasonable hysterical laughter, which often became so violent she fell to the floor.

This behavior went on for a few weeks until a sudden escalation one night at her home. Priscilla began screaming out in terrible pain, grabbing different parts of her body in terror. Her family didn't think much of her behavior, even when she grabbed at her throat choking, perhaps feeling it was a bid for attention. Though it was all too real to Priscilla.

MANIFESTATIONS

Soon Priscilla began experiencing seizures in which her body twisted and she was only able to say the words money, misery, and sin. Oddly enough, she was fully aware during the seizures, even able to repeat what others said in her presence. However, she still remained uncontrollable over her body as she thrashed around on the floor. Her long, blonde hair whipped through the air as her limbs twisted into unimaginable, painful contortions. This finally concerned her parents enough to contact the pastor. They all agreed this seemed to go beyond merely vying for attention.

Another abnormal fact of the seizures is they didn't seem to weaken her at all. She was stronger and more energetic after the seizure than she was before, which is quite the opposite of a purely physical seizure. Her strength became so omnipotent; it took almost six full-grown men to pin her down on the floor so she wouldn't hurt herself, especially near the open fireplace, a seemingly favorite target for whatever was controlling her body.

Besides having the ability to hear those around her, she could later identify people in the room though her eyes were clamped shut, even if the people were silent. The seizures would intensify when the pastor came into the room, though with her eyes closed she had no way of knowing he had entered.

MURDEROUS URGES

The seizures were not the worst part of Priscilla's experience. As her possession progressed, other strange symptoms manifested. In between seizures, she would leap around the house making animal sounds ranging from a barking dog to a bleating sheep. Additionally, she was overcome with murderous urges. It began with her parents, but then included her neighbors and the pastor's children she attended. Disturbingly, it was the youngest child that was the focus of most of her obsessions. These homicidal cravings were so strong it took all the will power she had remaining not to act on them. This, according to Priscilla, was one of the most frightening aspects of her experience.

When her symptoms worsened, she was taken to live at the pastor's home under the care of his family. One night after arriving, Priscilla awoke with the horrifying, homicidal impulse raging through her, as if her very blood was on fire. She couldn't get the idea out of her mind.

Weakened from months of fighting these battles, she gave in. With access to a billhook (sickle-like device), she silently crept out of bed and headed down the long hall to the pastor's bedroom. Convinced he was asleep, she was prepared to kill him; however, he was walking along the hall when he encountered a very strange acting Priscilla. She discreetly tucked the billhook out of sight beneath the folds of her gown and made an excuse for why she was in the hall. Frightened, yet relieved, she headed back to her room. Fortunately, the murderous urge had receded. It would be several weeks before the pastor found out how close he came to being murdered.

These murderous urges were not just limited to others, however. Many times Priscilla struggled with suicidal thoughts and impulses, going as far as to perch on the edge of a well preparing to jump in until something distracted her and the urge disappeared. She also fantasized about hanging herself, but never succeeded in fully putting those fantasies into action.

SATANIC VISITS AND PACTS

Priscilla finally revealed Satan had appeared to her multiple times while she was working and later living under the pastor's roof. It all started when she ventured into the pastor's cellar to retrieve some supplies. There, she saw two strange figures, but frightened, ran upstairs. She had someone else go down to the cellar with her, but they saw no one. This person did say, however, he noticed Priscilla talking with someone, though they were alone. Priscilla claimed her mistake was greeting the one she later believed to be Satan with the words, "What cheer, old man?" Apparently, a seemingly innocent greeting gave the evil being access to her mind and later her body.

According to her, Satan appeared to her multiple times. In his hand he always held a book filled with the contracts he made with individuals, signed in blood, and he wanted her to make a pact with him, also. Priscilla said he pointed out her discontent in life—living in a small town, being from a relatively poor family, having to work for the pastor, never having an any hope of seeing the world—and he promised her some very tempting things such as a chance to see the world, access to great wealth, fashionable clothes, and never having to work again.

Priscilla said she never made a league with the devil, but later statements seem to contradict that claim. She did admit he would often appear when she was the most discontented with her life—depressed, weary of her work, and longing for excitement. She also admitted she would listen to him, rather than fleeing from him, for he always seemed sympathetic of her plight.

Priscilla's claims would alternate between those of terror at the sight of the Devil to confessing of purposely staying late at work to go home after dark, thus having a better chance of encountering the Devil. He would appear to her in the shadows of darkness on her way home alone, walking, talking, and sympathizing with her in order to tempt her. She later confessed she had traveled with him on at least two occasions: she on horseback and he in the form of a large, menacing black dog that followed close behind.

The Devil wasn't the only being she saw; later on she stated that, to her horror, she had witnessed more demonic creatures than she had ever witnessed humans. These creatures were somewhat human in form, but loathsome, deformed, and mutated to the point they were horrifying to gaze upon. Not all of these demons merely appeared, either; some of them would bite her, strangle her, speak to her, and throw her down on the floor. Apparently, at least one of these creatures was visible to another young lady, too.

MEDICAL TREATMENTS

Many Christians in the community prayed and counseled Priscilla, including her pastor, but they all had the same question in mind: was Priscilla truly possessed?

A local physician was called to evaluate her and his initial opinion, based on the limited medical knowledge of the time, was her possession was due to stomach problems and bad blood. He went so far to say the bad blood caused dangerous fumes to collect in her brain, which was the source of all her problems.

He prescribed her a curative, which likely seems to have been some type of tranquilizer. The seizures grew less frequent and less intense and Priscilla was sent back home to her parents. Her problems were not over, however.

TROUBLES RETURN

Over time, her behavior became odd all over again and she began to alternate between being glad she was free of the demons and being sad she no longer had visits from them. Soon the seizures began again in force, exhibiting the same impossible contortions with the same awareness of her surroundings. This time, however, Priscilla couldn't speak at all: her tongue was arched up to the roof of her mouth. Her tongue would remain in that position for hours at a time, with even the strongest of men unable to dislodge it from this position. As her condition worsened, they called for the pastor again.

From that point, she began what can only be described as a descent into torment and madness. The seizures began to last for hours at a time and her behavior in between became more erratic and senseless. She had to be watched closely because of multiple suicide attempts, yet those watching her had to be careful because of her violent attacks upon them. When she did succeed in harming someone, she would laugh with devilish delight.

The pastor and Priscilla's family, it seems, had begun to doubt she was truly possessed. Priscilla would confess to something one day, then recant the next, and then confess something similar a few days later. They began to suspect this was all an attempt to gain attention, like her family believed at the very beginning. However, their minds would be changed.

INTERVENTION

One fateful Sunday, Priscilla's seizures started afresh, but suddenly her tongue was drawn so far out of her mouth it seemed physically impossible. Her body, very bloated and fleshy, began to bend and twist as if she were a circus contortionist. Then a new voice came forth from her lips. It was a deep, guttural, aggressive, masculine voice that mocked them for attending church that Sunday morning and called the pastor a loathsome liar.

The family immediately called for the pastor out of fear. When the pastor arrived, he was seriously taken aback. Nothing in Priscilla's behavior up to that time pointed so clearly to demonic possession. The pastor would later admit he was frightened, having never dealt with demon possession up close and personal and he could no longer deny the demonic overtones of what was happening.

Subsequently, the evil voice coming from Priscilla began to name those present and then list every secret, sinful act he or she had committed in the past, even those Priscilla had no way of knowing. This frightened many present, needless to say, and pointed once again toward demonic powers.

When confronted as to whom he was, the spirit answered, "I am a pretty boy and this is my pretty girl." This chilled Priscilla's parents to their very core—this evil thing was claiming their young daughter as its own property!

Those present began to pray for Priscilla's deliverance. She would become quiet during those times, but the instant they stopped praying that same demonic voice would begin to speak. The battle continued for several more days until everyone involved was worn out.

Over time, the seizures became less severe, but she never regained the ability to speak. The evil spirit eventually quit speaking through her and it only took one person to keep an eye on her for her own safety. Sadly, Priscilla never fully recovered.

JULIA: SATAN'S PRIESTESS

Dr. Richard Gallagher, a board-certified psychiatrist, published a paper entitled, "Among the Many Counterfeits, a Case of Demonic Possession," in *The Oxford Review* (March 2008) discussing his experiences with a patient whom he fully believed was demon possessed.

JULIA'S BACKGROUND

Julia, the pseudonym he used for his patient, was in her early forties; a self-supporting, intelligent woman whom he described as quite poised. In an informal conversation with her, there was nothing to hint she was controlled by anything paranormal and she seemed logical and quite sane. To all appearances, Julia was a normal, attractive, well-spoken woman. The main thing that did stand out about Julia was her rather dramatic choice of appearance: all black clothing combined with an abundance of dark eye makeup.

Julia was a self-styled satanic priestess who had been active in various satanic cults throughout the years. There was nothing to cause those involved in her case to doubt the truth of this, and even she admitted it was most likely the cause behind her possession.

She initially asked for help from the Catholic Church when her symptoms began to manifest. Being raised Catholic, though rejecting Catholicism in the past, she still felt it was her best hope. It was one of the priests working on her case that asked Dr. Gallagher to participate in her cause.

VOICES

Some of the chilling aspects of Julia's possession were the voices that would speak through her. They ranged from deep, guttural, and menacing to abnormally high-pitched. All of the voices were markedly different from Julia's normal speaking voice, as well as her normal means of expression. The voices would claim ownership of Julia and mock those trying to help her using filthy, scatological language. These voices expressed an unbelievable level of hatred and vitriol besides knowing disturbing things about those in the vicinity of Julia.

These voices didn't only speak English, as Julia did; they were fluent in Spanish, Latin, and Greek. It seemed they relished distracting the priests and nuns involved by utilizing classical languages. The voices were always crude and abusive, punctuating their threats with foul language. None of this was typical of Julia's pattern of speech or the content of her conversations; neither the tone of voice, speech patterns, or expressions in any way reflected Julia.

CLAIRVOYANCE

In one incident, Julia mentioned to a team member, "Those cats really had a fight last night, didn't they?" Most may not find this statement out of context; however, the team member lived in a different city than Julia and had been awaked at 2 a.m. by her two pet cats, who normally got along very well, having a terrible cat fight. Apparently whatever was in control of Julia knew about it and might have even instigated it. This event was, to say the least, quite intimidating, which was no doubt the purpose behind it.

In another instance, Julia spoke to another team member about his/her deceased family member, with information concerning their relationship, personality, and the type of cancer suffering. Julia had no previous information concerning the team member's family. Once again, whatever was controlling Julia was trying to intimidate those working for her deliverance.

Julia would often reveal to team members their secret weaknesses and sins in addition to accurately stating the location and actions of people called to work on the case – before she ever met them. Members believe something wanted the team to know there was nothing about them it didn't know.

During her exorcisms, Julia could tell the difference between holy water and plain tap water. If plain tap water was poured or sprinkled on her, she showed no physical reaction; however, if holy water was applied to her she would scream out as in extreme pain.

TECHNOLOGY

The voices speaking through Julia didn't just limit themselves to evaluation and exorcism times. In a quite chilling episode, Dr. Gallagher was discussing Julia's case on the phone with a priest far from where Julia was located. In the middle of the conversation, one of Julia's demonic voices interrupted the conversation, ordering the men to leave Julia alone. Both men were completely baffled as to how her voice managed to come over the phone line as well as how it knew they were discussing her at that time.

LEVITATION

What did impress the team, however, was how Julia would sometimes levitate during exorcisms. In one particular instance, a group of witnesses, including health professionals and nuns working as psychiatric nurses, saw Julia floating unsupported about 10 inches above the floor for thirty minutes. This was not the only time she was said to have levitated, but it was the most impressive instance and occurred during an attempted exorcism.

Levitation was not the most dramatic manifestation associated with Julia's condition. During another levitation incident, while suspended in the air six inches off the floor, objects began to fly off shelves around the room in a terrifying display of what experts call psychokinesis. Oddly enough, when Julia was questioned about the incident later on she did not remember any of it.

TRANCES

When levitating or speaking in these other voices, Julia would go into a trance-like state. It was as if she checked out and something "else" checked in.

During these trances, besides manifesting paranormal powers, Julia would speak of herself in the third-person and much of what was said took the form of taunts, jeers, and threats. Phrases such as "She's ours!", "Leave her alone, imbecile!", and other expressions peppered with extreme profanity were quite common. Another characteristic of what was said was a very great contempt for religion and all things sacred, going so far as to call the nuns "whores." She also exhibited superhuman strength to the point at least three women held her down so she wouldn't harm herself of others.

EXORCISM

One a warm, sunny day, Julia was brought in for another exorcism. As she was led into the room, those present felt a dramatic, icy drop in temperature; it was an unnatural cold that chilled them to bone as the room took on an eerie, hostile atmosphere. Nevertheless, when the demons began to speak through Julia things changed dramatically. The temperature in the room consistently increased and those working with her began to sweat profusely as the temperatures continued to rise to almost unbearable levels.

As they continued with prayers and rituals, in spite of the stifling, unnatural heat, the sounds coming from Julia changed to chilling animalistic uproars, seemingly impossible for any human being to make. Soon the voices switched back to their normal behavior, utilizing different languages to pour forth abuse, contempt, and sacrilege with extreme hatred and anger.

Sadly, while the exorcisms proved to be helpful, Julia never found complete freedom from the demons that possessed her.

MICHAEL TAYLOR: FROM EXORCISM TO MURDER

Michael Taylor, husband of Christine Taylor and father of five children, was a butcher in Ossett, England. He and his family seemed like a typical family of the 1970s; he was quite happily married, loved his children, and he did not suffer from depression or other mental issues. He was an average looking 30-year old man with a big smile and laidback personality, though he did have chronic back pain. His young wife, Christine, was an attractive blonde and seemed quite attached to him.

Their quiet life took a disturbing turn, though, when Michael became involved with a local religious sect called The Christian Fellowship Group. He and his family were not at all religious until a neighbor invited him to attend one of the meetings. There he met the lay leader of the group, 22-year old Marie Robinson, and he became obsessed with both the group and her.

RELIGION AND ADULTERY

This group, later described as a cult by some involved, soon took up much of Michael's time. He began to attend all the services, participate in deliverance-type meetings, and attend personal prayer meetings with Marie. He was also spending less and less time at home and when he was at home, things seemed very different. Christine, who was beginning to suspect that there was more to Michael and Marie's relationship than just prayer, became very concerned.

She began to wonder if he was having an affair with Marie. Later on, Michael stated he remembers suddenly appearing naked in front of Marie and feeling evil stirring within him. He claimed her eyes turned to slits and she seduced him. He tried to fight it, he said, but the temptation overcame him. He claimed he went to her seeking knowledge and spiritual guidance, but in retrospect he could see this was not the right way and felt betrayed.

Marie, however, told quite a different story. She said she was visiting Michael at his home and as Christine left the room, Michael kissed Marie. Marie rejected his advances, reminding him of how much he loved his wife. He agreed and when Christine came back in the room he informed her that a great victory had been won because he and Marie had overcome their passions.

CONFRONTATION

Either way, it's very clear something was quite wrong with Michael's thinking. According to those who knew him best, this was simply not the Michael they knew; there had been a drastic change in his behavior, and it wasn't good. On top of everything else, he lost his job and was suffering severe depression.

Christine, his 29-year old wife and mother of his children, began to worry about him more and more. Finally, she could not take any more and took matters into her own hands. During a religious service she openly, before the congregation, accused Michael of cheating on her with Marie. She expected Michael to react with anger, no doubt, but she never could have expected what happened next.

Normally laid-back, mellow Michael turned with a primal fury, not on Christine, but on Marie. According to witnesses, his facial features twisted into something downright bestial as he jumped to his feet and charged toward her, yelling obscenities and screaming at her in different languages. Enraged, he slapped her brutally on the face. Marie said the look out of his eyes convinced her he wanted to kill her and she was frightened for her life. Several members of the group leaped to their feet to grab hold of Michael before he could harm Marie further, though it took awhile for them to restrain him.

Michael continued to yell and scream at Marie, switching from language to language. Terrified, both Marie and Christine began to call on the name of Jesus. As they did, Michael calmed down enough to be released. After it was all over, Michael insisted he had no memory of what happened.

PERSONALITY SHIFT

Michael returned to the next meeting and seemingly the group, including Marie, forgave him. Conversely, things were not well at home. Even before the incident, Christine noticed his behavior changing.

He was irritable, angry, and sullen, and when he was home he seemed to stifle the joy from their existence. In public, he was doing strange things like spitting on people and telling them it was the milk of human kindness. Even the neighbors noticed the usually boisterous, laughing family was abnormally quiet and reserved.

EXORCISM

As his behavior became more and more erratic, someone talked to a local Anglican priest. Based on what he heard, the priest decided an exorcism was needed.

Both Anglican and Methodist ministers were called in to assist with the exorcism, which Michael agreed to participate in.

Michael and his young wife met with the exorcism team, which lasted all night and into the morning. During the process, Michael had convulsions along with screaming, biting, scratching, and spitting. He was tied to the floor for the safety of all. Anytime someone came near Michael, he would snarl and snap at them like a wild animal.

The prayers, confessions, and Bible readings went on for hours while Michael fought, seeming to be more animalistic than human at times. By early the next morning, the team claimed they had cast 40 demons out of Michael, including demons of incest, bestiality, blasphemy, and lewdness. Worn out, the group decided to stop and try again a bit later because they felt there were three demons left: demons of insanity, murder, and violence.

The wife of one of the ministers was present at the exorcism and she felt very, very strongly if the team let Michael go, he would most certainly kill Christine. She spoke to her husband and begged the team to keep at it a little longer and not leave such a crucial, dangerous job unfinished. Unfortunately, the exhausted team ignored her words, which proved to be prophetic.

PROPHECY FULFILLED

Michael returned home with Christine to rest up for another exorcism. Within two hours of their return, Christine was dead.

Michael strangled her with his hands. Then, while apparently naked, he had pried out her eyeballs, ripped out her tongue, and tore most of her face off, all with his bare hands and fingernails. Autopsy reports showed she died quickly, but had inhaled some of her own blood. Fortunately, the children were not at home when this took place, but police also found Michael's mother-in-law's pet poodle strangled and torn almost limb from limb. The crime scene was disturbing to even the most experienced officers on the local police force who struggled with the memories for years. The officers described Christine as simply torn to pieces.

The murder was discovered after Michael was found wandering the streets, naked and covered in blood, crying, "It's the Devil's blood! It's the Devil's blood!" Officers took him into custody and the crime scene was discovered when they went to his home to check on his wife.

Michael had become convinced Christine was the demon possessed, confessing to officers later, "Released. I am released. It is done. The evil in her has been destroyed." It seemed the demons remained in control of him, with the only way for Michael and Christine to be free was for Christine to die.

The minister's wife was correct: those demons of violence, insanity, and murder were aiming to see Christine destroyed.

AFTERMATH

Michael was tried for murder, but was acquitted on the grounds of insanity. He attempted suicide four times and spent two years in a mental hospital, then two years in a secure ward. Years after his release, Michael was arrested and tried for inappropriately touching an underage girl. He was found guilty and less than a year into his sentence it was noted that he was exhibiting the same type of behavior he had shortly before Christine's murder. He was once again remanded into psychiatric care.

It is speculated he was never fully freed of the demons that drove him to murder his wife and leave his five children motherless with what many perceived to be a monster for a father, proving demon possession doesn't just affect the possessed.

MASS POSSESSION AT THE ELSA PEREA FLORE SCHOOL

There are many names applied to what happened at a Peruvian middle school in 2016: mass hysteria, contagious demon possession, and/or demonic interference. Initial media reports stated the children were suffering from a contagious condition, but no medical explanation was ever found.

SUDDEN ONSET

It began when about 20 children, ages 11 to 14, fell violently ill at about the same time at Colegio Elsa Perea Flore School in Tarapoto, Peru about two months after their school year started. These students, in different classes, were going through their typical daily routine when they began to have convulsions and seizures, followed by delirium, hearing voices, nausea, vomiting, foaming at the mouth, and fainting.

Eventually, 100 children fell victim to the same symptoms, often fainting almost simultaneously while in different classrooms. The number of children that fell ill at the same time caused them to be carried to the hospital in trucks rather than ambulances.

Once they arrived at the hospital, doctors and nurses could only treat the symptoms because they had no idea of the cause. Their only recourse was to label it a case of mass hysteria.

MEDIA COVERAGE

The pictures shared by the media at the time were disturbing: middle-aged school children, in matching plaid uniforms and white knee socks, all in various stages of illness and terror. Some of the images showed the children being carried out of the school by worried doctors and nurses.

Other pictures show children pinned down to the desks, friends and faculty trying to restrain them to prevent them from hurting themselves out of fear and delirium. One image depicts a dark-haired young girl, her head cradled by an adult as her eyes fixated on something no one else saw while her mouth was spread open in a chilling scream.

TALL, DARK MAN

What was scaring these children so much was not the symptoms of the illness, as frightening as those may have been; the source of terror was a common vision all the children affected by this paranormal outbreak experienced: a tall, bearded man.

All the children expressed being chased by a tall man with a big beard and dressed in dark clothing, intent on making physical contact with them—a touch they instinctively feared. The children claimed he relentlessly chased them, yet during those times everyone around them testified they were seemingly unconscious, but screaming in utter terror.

SOURCE

The cause of this outbreak remains unclear. Some people claim it began after a handful of students used an Ouija board in an attempt to communicate with ghosts that haunted the school. Authorities or religious figures never verified this.

Another possibility lies in the story that during the construction of the school, human remains were uncovered. Despite the discovery of what many believed to be a mass grave used by the local Mafia, construction went forward. Could this graveyard, over which the school was built, be the focal point for the problem?

CONCLUSION: UNKNOWN

School officials and parents called in every expert known from medical doctors and researchers to holy men, priests, and exorcists (who carried out masses on the campus). Nothing seemed to relieve the problems. For two months, this paranormal epidemic spread throughout the school, then seemed to die out as mysteriously as it started.

Fortunately, each student recovered quite quickly. A visit to the school's Facebook page seems to show everything has returned to normal...for now.

DAVID:
THE BEAST MAN AND THE BOY

David was about 11-years old when his family began renovating some new property. One fateful day, while the family was busy remodeling this older house, David's mother saw him suddenly fall backwards onto the bed for no obvious reason. Naturally she asked him what happened and his reply was rather puzzling: "The old man pushed me."

THE OLD MAN

When pressed, David told his mother he had been pushed onto the bed by an old man dressed in jeans and a flannel shirt. He had a very white beard, but his skin was rough as if it had been burned. He said that after the old man pushed him down, he pointed a long, skinny finger at his chest and simply said, "Beware!" His mother saw nothing and decided David was just trying to avoid work.

It turns out, this was just the beginning of a season of absolute terror for young David.

NIGHTMARES COME TO LIFE

Next, David began to have nightmares in which he saw what he called "The Beast Man." This creature looked somewhat like a tall, dark man at first glance, but his eyes were large and completely black, his feet formed hooves, his facial features were animalistic, his ears were tall and pointed, his teeth were jagged, and he had horns extending from his head.

David said this creature would appear in his nightmares and was after his soul. His mother was concerned about these recurring nightmares that caused David to wake up screaming, but things got even worse. After the nightmares, she would find bruises and scratch marks on David that had no natural explanation and seemingly appeared on him while he slept.

Imagine David's horror when The Beast Man began to appear during the daytime! Not only that, but imagine the family's fear when deep scratch marks began to appear on the front door just around the time David told them he saw The Beast Man in the house.

ODD NOISES

The situation escalated even further when mysterious noises began to descend from the attic. Debbie, David's older sister, asked her boyfriend Cheyenne to stay with the family to help out with David. When the noises would begin, Cheyenne would quickly make his way to the attic, only to discover nothing that could possibly be causing the mysterious sounds.

PROGRESSION

As things continued, David's personality began to change and his nightmares grew much worse. Eventually someone had to stay up with him all night because he would go into convulsions about every thirty minutes. In addition, he gained almost 60 pounds in just a few months, despite the loss of sleep, convulsions, and high stress levels he was under.

DEMONIC MANIFESTATIONS

A priest was called in to perform a blessing on the home, but it seemed to intensify David's problems. More noises exerted from the attic, as did increased daytime appearances of The Beast Man and the old man, too. David began to exhibit very disturbing behavior, such as hearing voices no one else heard and growling. David began to kick, bite, and swear using words his family didn't even know he knew. He would also growl and hiss, some kind of beast instead of a young boy. He didn't seem like David anymore.

David began to quote verbatim from Milton's *Paradise Lost*, hardly reading material for an eleven-year old boy and certainly not among David's preferred reading. He also began to speak in strange voices and quoted Latin.

THE WARRENS

Ed and Lorraine Warren, well-known demonologists, were called in to see if there was anything they could do to identify the source of the problem and help David.

Lorraine identified an evil presence in pursuit of David. As David sat at the family kitchen table during his initial interview with the Warrens, Lorraine saw a very dark, ominous mist take form beside David. Moments later, David said he was being strangled and enormous, red bruises appeared on his neck where no bruising had been moments before. The Warrens were certain that a demonic entity was involved.

EXORCISM

Four priests were summoned and a series of three unofficial exorcisms were performed. During the exorcisms, David would growl, hiss, thrash, kick, fight, and spit like a wild animal. Strange voices, making horrific claims and prophecies, would speak through him. According to the Warrens, there were 43 demons cast out of young David.

After the exorcisms, David began to improve dramatically. The noises in the attic stopped, as did the convulsions and nightmares. The Beast Man wasn't through with this family yet, though.

CHEYENNE: THE BEAST MAN AND THE NICE GUY

Cheyenne was a 19-year-old young man with a reputation for working hard for those he loved. He had quit school before he graduated to help his family and even purchased an old clunker of a car for his mother so she wouldn't have to walk back and forth to work.

This well-liked, blonde-headed nice guy with the muscular, compact build would do just about anything for anybody; when he found out his girlfriend's little brother David was going through some scary things, he was more than happy to move in with the family and provide whatever help he could.

DAVID'S EXORCISM AND A SERIOUS MISTAKE

Cheyenne was there when the priests were performing exorcisms on David, whom he had come to love like his own little brother. During one of these exorcisms, though, Cheyenne made a very serious mistake. In his misguided concern for David, he challenged the demons to "leave the little guy alone" and come into him instead.

At the time, it seemed like nothing had happened, but demonologist Lorraine Warren knew there could be serious repercussions for Cheyenne. She even went so far as to warn the local police that there might be problems and asked them to please keep an eye on Cheyenne.

TRANCES AND CHANGES

Before long, Cheyenne and his girlfriend, Debbie, were engaged and decided to get their own place. Debbie was able to get a job for a local dog groomer and kennel owner named Alan, who was about 40-years old. Alan owned an apartment next to the kennel and offered to rent it to Debbie and Cheyenne. They took him up on his offer, and it seemed that things were going well…for a while.

Debbie noticed Cheyenne started to go into trances, in which he search around and growl at something Debbie couldn't see. This immediately reminded Debbie of what happened to her little brother, David. She also remembered that one of the voices that came through David said The Beast Man would enter Cheyenne and cause him to murder someone. Debbie recalled David swore he saw The Beast Man enter Cheyenne's body.

As soon as the trance was over, Debbie confronted Cheyenne about what was going on, but he had no memory of anything happening; it was as if the trance was simply lost time. Debbie was horrified, but there was nothing she could do. Suddenly, Cheyenne began to have run-ins with the local police, though he did not have a police record or had ever been in trouble with the law.

LANDLORD'S LAST DAY

One fateful day, Cheyenne decided to call in sick to his job where he worked as a tree surgeon. He decided he would spend the day with Debbie and his sister, Wanda, as they worked in the kennel. As the morning wore on, Debbie's nine-year old cousin Mary arrived. Together, the little group was enjoying the company of the dogs and chatting.

Around lunchtime, Debbie's boss and landlord, Alan, showed up and took them all out to lunch at a local bar. Alan and Cheyenne got very drunk and as they returned to the kennel Debbie began to get a very bad feeling.

As she was trying to decide what to do about this feeling, Cheyenne and Alan began to argue. The argument quickly escalated and Cheyenne started growling and hissing at Alan. His behavior was becoming more beast-like by the minute.

Knowing something very bad was about to happen, Debbie was prepared to pull Wanda and Mary out of the room. She managed to grasp Wanda's arm, but when Alan saw they were going to leave the room he grabbed the arm little nine-year-old Mary and refused to let go of her.

MURDER

Cheyenne pulled out a 5-inch folding pocketknife from his pocket and stabbed Alan in the stomach. Instead of pulling the knife out, he pulled it upward to Alan's heart. Debbie rushed the others out of the room as Cheyenne began repeatedly stabbing Alan in the chest and stomach before running away.

AFTERMATH

The police arrived and Alan died several hours later. The doctors were horrified at the gaping wound that extended from below his stomach up to his heart. They also noted four other very large wounds on his body and a total of 40 stab wounds.

The police apprehended Cheyenne about two miles from the crime scene. Needless to say, Cheyenne was tried for murder and when lawyers attempted to get him off on the claim he was demon possessed, the trial became known as the "Demon Murder Trial."

The judge refused to allow Cheyenne to make a plea based on demon possession and the trial proceeded as a normal murder trial despite the media circus that quickly surrounded it. Cheyenne was convicted and served five years of a ten to twenty-year sentence. He and Debbie and now happily married and it seems that The Beast Man went his way.

ANNA: MOST UNNATURAL

Moments after the exorcism began, teenager Anna slid loose from the restraints holding her to the cast iron bed frame and jumped up from the mattress, hanging from the bare wall above the doorway. Those present could find no natural explanation of how she managed to hang with only her hands and feet, nor could they explain why it took so much combined strength to pull her back down.

They also couldn't provide a natural explanation of how she saw where to leap because her eyes were clamped tightly shut as soon as the exorcism began. Additionally, they could not explain the multitude of voices emerging from her when her lips were firmly fastened. Anna couldn't shed any light on the situation because she endured a trance-like state during the exorcisms, remembering nothing when fully conscious.

BACKGROUND

Anna had been a very devout, well-behaved 14-year old girl with a spotless reputation when things began to go seriously wrong for her. It is believed her parents, who dabbled in witchcraft, cursed her. To this day, no one knows exactly why she became possessed.

It began with her sudden inability to participate in religious activities that had been such a major part of her life: prayer, attending mass, confession, reading the Bible, and taking sacrament. Anna described unseen hands holding her back from participating in these activities.

Anna was utterly terrified as the activities that were so meaningful and comforting were forcibly torn away from her by something as she gradually lost more and more control over her own actions.

From there, things increasingly worsened. Anna began to hear inner voices suggesting things to her she found utterly abhorrent and often blasphemous. The voices and attacks on her mind grew relentless and tried to get her to do things like attack her spiritual adviser or shatter her holy water font. Anna thought she was going insane.

When things reached a breaking point in her later teens and an exorcism was approved by the Catholic Church. A priest in the town of Earling, Iowa was asked to allow the exorcism to take place in his parish. Due to the stigma associated with demon possession, the church wanted to help the girl keep her identity a secret. The priest agreed to have the exorcism take place and a group of nuns in the area kindly volunteered their convent as the site of the exorcism.

THE NIGHTMARE BEGINS

When Anna arrived in Earling, she later said she had an almost irrepressible urge to choke the very life out of those who were there to help her, even though she desperately wanted to be free of the demons within her and she appreciated their kindness and sacrifice.

The very night Anna arrived at the convent, the nuns realized first-hand they were dealing with something beyond this world. One of the nuns prepared Anna's dinner with holy water; Anna violently reacted to the food and refused to eat it. She instead sat down in a chair and began to make a sound like the purring of a large, menacing, cat. Another meal was prepared for her, without holy water, before she would eat. This was the last full meal Anna ate until the exorcism process was complete.

THE EXORCISM

The exorcism began the next morning after the team managed to pull Anna down from the wall. Once she was again secured to the bed for everyone's safety, they heard a large pack of wild animals growling threateningly. The sound was jarringly unnatural, as if it were coming from a far-off place. It seemed to be the war cry of the demons that had taken possession of Anna though Anna's mouth and lips remained tightly clamped.

VOICES AND SOUNDS

All through the exorcism, various animal sounds could be heard. The sounds ranged from a large group of dogs barking and howling to hyenas, cats, and cattle. It seemed as if whatever was possessing Anna was determined to unnerve those present, but they also managed to alert those in the town of an exorcism going on at the convent.

Animalistic inflections were not the only noises resonating from the room; numerous voices came from Anna's tightly sealed lips. Some voices were human, deep like a man's voice or high-pitched like a woman's voice. Others were bestial, filled with unbelievable rage while others echoed utter hopelessness and unbearable grief. Not one of the voices bore any resemblance to Anna's natural, youthful voice.

The voices spoke and understood languages Anna had never even heard growing up in rural Iowa. For example, when blessed in Latin, "she" would begin to foam at the mouth and become enraged. The possessed Anna would also correct and mock the priests when they would mispronounce some of the Latin words in the rites and prayers.

Often, the priests would address the demons in German and Latin and the demonic voices would reply accordingly, understanding perfectly what was being said.

VOMIT

Those participating in her 23-day exorcism could not explain how she could vomit buckets-full of vile fluid 10-20 times a day when she barely consumed any beverages at all. It wasn't always just fluids, either. In one instance, she vomited up something similar to macaroni and another time it was sliced tobacco leaves, yet she hadn't consumed any solid food in days.

Sometimes she would spit this mysterious fluid at those trying to help her and other times she would cough it up. Most of the time, though, it came out as projectile vomit. The priest leading the exorcism constantly wiped down his vestment, for it seemed to be aimed in his direction most of the time.

STRANGE OCCURENCES

All through the exorcism, the priests involved struggled with unexplained problems, from mysterious sounds keeping them awake at night to car troubles even mechanics could not find. There were also problems in their respective parishes including a dramatic increase in misunderstandings with parishioners and unrest in their congregations.

PHYSICAL MANIFESTATIONS

The exorcism team noted Anna's pitiful physical appearance as the exorcism progressed. Her face become so distorted she was unrecognizable. Her body remained twisted and disfigured even when she wasn't in the thrall of convulsions, with those present claiming it wasn't shaped like a normal body. She grew more and more emaciated and had to be fed liquids with a feeding tube.

Ironically, during the exorcisms her normally tiny, frail body would suddenly bloat to such an enormous size it seemed just touching her would cause her to burst, yet later on it would go back to normal. The bloating caused her weight to suddenly increase, causing the iron legs of the bed frame to bow outwards, and her abdomen and extremities were as hard as a rock. One can only imagine the havoc this must have wreaked on her body.

Anna lost so much weight her head appeared too large for her slender body. Her bulging eyes were reddened with a seemingly glowing expression while her lips were unnaturally swollen, split open, and protruded from her mouth in a most pitiful manner. It seemed unlikely Anna would physically survive the exorcism process.

VISIONS

When Anna was resting from the exorcisms, she would have terrifying visions of battles between the powers of darkness and the powers of light. She also had a vision of a cluster of white roses on the ceiling, which was also visible to some of the nuns in her room at the time. A different type of vision, of pure kindness and hope spoke to her and encouraged her she would come through the exorcism. This was promising to Anna and the exorcism team who had been working so hard to see her freed.

VICTORY

As already mentioned, the exorcism went on for a total of 23 days, though it was ten days before any discernible progress was made. The exorcists encountered multiple demons, some far more aggressive and stronger than others. The demons hated all things related to Christianity and had a special antipathy towards the priests and the mother superior of the convent. Day after day, the demons tormented Anna and the exorcism team fought through the vomit, repulsive odors, blasphemy, vitriol, and horrific sounds that filled the room for over three weeks.

Finally, on the 23rd day, something wonderful happened—with a sudden jerk, Anna was on her feet. She had pulled away from those holding her down on the mattress and was standing with just her heels touching the bed. As quickly as she stood, she collapsed back onto the mattress.

A piercing, echoing sound could be heard repeating the names the demons had given to the priests, adding the words, "To Hell, Hell, Hell." Anna's eyes and mouth opened and her voice spoke forth from behind a smile: "From what a terrible burden I have been freed at last! My, Jesus, Mercy! Praise be to Jesus Christ!"

Anna was delivered and never troubled by demons again.

BILL RAMSEY: A REAL WEREWOLF?

Bill Ramsey was a compactly built, slightly balding, middle-aged Englishman with an unassuming personality. He stood at about 5'7" and weighed around 150 pounds. He made a living as a carpenter and had a wife and three kids he loved. At first glance, there was nothing particularly striking about him; nevertheless, his calm exterior hid a secret for many years—demon possession.

FIRST MANIFESTATION

Bill's problems first appeared when he was a little tyke of nine-years old in 1952. Bill had just returned from the movies and said his mind was filled with images of Royal Air Force fighters and heroes. He was playing in the garden behind his home when a strange feeling, both physical and mental, swept over him. His skin felt icy cold and a vile, vomit-inducing stench filled his nostrils and sinuses. As she stood there, all other thoughts were pushed out of his mind except two: running away and wolves.

Bill suddenly fell to the ground. In fear and confusion, he cried out for his mother who heard him from within the house. Before his mother and father reached him, he lost control of his mind, emotions, and body. Something else filled him that carried with it an uncontrollable, senseless rage. As that rage filled his mind, adrenaline seemed to fill his tiny body and he stood to his feet. He turned and grabbed onto the first thing he saw—a wooden fence post. To his parents' utter shock, he pulled it completely out of the ground with the fence still attached. This feat of strength was unbelievable to his parents and neither one of them could recreate this act with the same ease with which Bill had accomplished it.

Next, he began to swing that same fence post with a vengeance. When his parents caught up to him, he suddenly dropped the fence post, tore the wire meshing from it, and began to chew on the mesh.

This scared both of Bill's parents so severely they instantly retreated into the house. As he gnawed on the fencing, Bill later said the same bitterly cold sensation swept across his skin again as a growl came from deep within him.

After a while, he calmed down and seemed to be back to normal. He knocked politely at the back door of his house, asking his puzzled parents to let him inside. The family did not speak of the incident again for many years.

NIGHTMARES

Much later in life after Bill married, he began to have trouble with recurring nightmares. In his nightmares, he would be just a couple of steps behind his wife who would turn, look Bill in the face, and she would take off running from him as terror gripped her facial features. Bill would immediately awaken at that moment, each time drenched in a cold sweat and his mind clouded with an impending sense of dread. These same dreams went on for two years.

NIGHTMARES COME TO LIFE

One night, after the nightmares had stopped, Bill had a very, very different type of dream. In his dream, he awoke in the middle of the night to the heavy panting of a wild animal in his bedroom. Only a few seconds later, as Bill threw the heaviness of sleep from his mind, he realized he was the animal. To Bill's great relief, it would be about 15 years before any other strange episodes happened to him.

THE WEREWOLF IN THE BACK SEAT

The next incident that occurred began in an English pub where Bill was drinking with friends. Suddenly, that familiar icy cold sensation whipped over him, just like it had when he was a boy. Knowing something was wrong, he quickly excused himself and headed straight for the bathroom.

There, as he leaned over the sink and looked into the smudged mirror, he didn't recognize what he saw. He expected to see his reflection, but instead he saw a wolf staring back into his soul. He shook his head, as if to shake the image out of his mind, and headed back to his friends. The cold feeling had dissipated and he decided all was well. But it wasn't.

Bill and a friend sat in the back seat on the car ride home. Unexpectedly, Bill lost control of himself, slowly growling and turning to his friend to viciously bite his leg. The very calm driver pulled over to the side of the road, got out, and started to try to get Bill out of the car.

Bill wasn't having it and seemed to be caught in some sort of maelstrom of rage. After several minutes of struggling, Bill calmed down and seemed perfectly normal again.

THE WEREWOLF AND THE HOSPITAL

Nothing more happened for about a year and a half, until one day Bill started to have chest pains, fearing he might be having a heart attack. He went to the local emergency room and was in the middle of having his blood pressure checked when that same old feeling swept over him.

Instantly he changed. The nurses and staff described the physical changes that swept over him: his shoulders hunched forward, his hands and fingers began to curl into the shape of claws, and he bared his teeth like an animal. Bill was no longer himself; something inhumane had taken his place—and it was angry.

He lunged for one of the nearby nurses and caught her near the elbow with his teeth, sinking them in as deep as he could. Next, he shoved everyone out of his way and went racing through the hospital, growling and animal-like with blood dripping from his mouth. Several people tried to stop him only to be thrown aside by what seemed to be superhuman strength.

It would take a team of people to pin Bill down long enough for the police to get handcuffs on him and tranquilize him.

THE WEREWOLF AND THE HOSPITAL, PART TWO

By the next morning, Bill was his normal self; on the advice of a doctor, he voluntarily checked himself into a mental hospital for observation. He stayed for a short time, but didn't experience any more symptoms and checked himself out.

In less than two months, Bill was back at the same hospital with more chest pains after a visit with his mother. Everything appeared fine until the nurse informed Bill she was going to find a doctor to assist him and Bill instantly became violent, throwing people aside and the like.

Four police officers showed up and, to their shock, Bill dropped on all fours like a canine and began growling, snarling, and snapping. Bill severely injured one of the officers causing him to remain hospitalized for four days. By the time the other officers placed Bill in the back of their squad car, he was back to normal again. After being released from the police station, Bill continued on without any problems for quite some time.

THE WEREWOLF AND THE POLICEMEN

The next time the police encountered Bill he voluntarily headed to the local police station to ask them to lock him up before he hurt someone as he had done the nurse and officer in the past. Bill was very much afraid he would end up going beyond just hurting someone and actually succeed in killing him or her.

An officer, much larger in size than Bill, approached Bill's car just as he was losing control of himself. The officer described Bill as having wide, staring eyes and a maniacal expression on his face. Bill told the officer, "The devil is in me and when the devil is in me I am strong. I am going to kill you. I am strong and you are going to die."

This burly, tall, muscular cop ended up on the ground with the smaller-sized Bill sitting on his chest and choking the life out of him. When other police officers tried to restrain him, he threw them off like they were nothing more than matchsticks (in their own words). It would take six police officers to apprehend Bill this time. His appearance during this fracas was described by police as that of a "mad dog."

Once they had him inside a cell, they were horrified beyond belief as they saw Bill forced his head and right arm (up to his shoulder) out of a narrow slot in the door, snarling and growling the entire time. It was physically impossible for a normal human being to do that, but police involved testified to this incident in the police reports regarding Bill Ramsey.

A doctor was called in to sedate Bill and allow officers to get his arm and head back out of the slot without harming Bill. No charges were made and Bill was released into a mental hospital where they ran tests for 28 days. Unable to find any problems with him, Bill was once again released.

Bill began to fear he would eventually end up in prison or a mental hospital for the rest of his life, in spite of all the doctors and psychiatrists had tried to help him.

THE WARRENS

Bill's story made the news and eventually reached Bill and Lorraine Warren, well-known ghost hunters and demonologists. Lorraine felt certain after reading about his situation his was a case of demon possession and that she and her husband could help Bill find freedom from this awful curse. She was determined to help Bill, even though she had never even met him.

The Warrens managed to find Bill and use their contacts to arrange an exorcism for Bill in the United States. Bill and his wife flew to the US and joined the Warrens in Connecticut. The night before the exorcism took place, Bill found himself trying to strangle his wife while she slept. Fortunately for all involved, he did not succeed.

The exorcism began with Bill strapped securely into a chair surrounded by six bodyguards armed with stun guns, in case anything went wrong and Bill got loose. The exorcist, Bishop McKenna, placed his hand on Bill's head. Bill said he felt as if he had been hit with a hammer and remembered nothing after that point; witnesses described Bill going into a trance-like state. For the first thirty minutes of the exorcism, it seemed nothing was happening.

Suddenly, however, Bill changed into a werewolf in front of everyone's eyes. The muscles in the back of Bill's neck began to enlarge, his ears twisted into a pointed shape, and a bone-chilling howl escaped his lips. Rage and fury seemed to pour forth out of him as he raised his hands up level with his face and his fingers twisted into claws. His lips pulled back, baring his white teeth and he began to growl and snarl as he had done in the hospital and the police station.

Bishop McKenna cast out the demon in Jesus' name. Bill relaxed; his face returned to normal; as he came out of the exorcism, he said he felt like a brand-new person. All nightmares and manifestations ceased and he has been able to live a quiet, peaceful life.

CLARA GERMANA CELE: SNAKE GIRL

Clara was a Bantu orphan who grew up at St. Michael's Mission in Natal, South Africa. She was described as a well-behaved, healthy, normal teenager with a bit of a whimsical streak. She certainly had no reputation for evil, nor was she in any way out of the ordinary—except for a tendency toward physical illness.

As far back as she could remember, Clara grew up in a very religious atmosphere, surrounded by nuns (who raised her from infancy) and priests and positive influences. However, on one fateful day, Clara made a serious mistake; according to her own confession, she made a pact with the Devil.

IT BEGINS

Clara began to be overtaken by impulses completely foreign to her, experienced fits of unbridled rage, and her language became increasingly foul and blasphemous. She changed so drastically, those around her could not help but take notice. The nuns tried to help her by giving her holy medals and praying for her, but it was not enough.

A BROKEN PACT

The night she made that confession, she was in a terribly confused and erratic state. She had frantically called for some of the sisters to come to her room. When they arrived, they beheld a terrified Clara in torn clothes, next to her bedframe, which she had broken with her bare hands. Clara cried out, "Get the priest! I have to confess something! Get him quickly! I am afraid Satan will kill me before I have a chance to confess!"

Wild and hysterical, she ransacked the room and cried out to a figure no else could see, "You betrayed me! You promised me glory and now you torture me!" She continued carrying on conversations with entities only visible to Clara.

The priest came to hear her confession and initially thought it was merely the theatrics of a teenage girl.

When paranormal manifestations began, however, he was quickly forced to change his mind. Before long, he realized Clara was most definitely demon possessed.

PHYSICAL MANIFESTATIONS

One of the manifestations the nuns found most disturbing was her incredible strength when under the influence of the demons possessing her. The nuns tried to restrain her to prevent her from hurting herself or others, but were hurled across the room as if they weighed next to nothing. Clara's behavior was likened to "savage bestiality" as she raged, snarling and growling while fighting tooth and nail. Some of the sisters ended up seriously injured as a result of her senseless wrath.

When in the throes of one of her spells, she would emit a sound resembling a herd of wild animals in "a choir led by Satan himself," according to one of the nuns. The sound was hair-raising, unearthly, loud, and difficult to forget.

Clara could also levitate at times, floating up to 5 feet above her bed, the first instance occurring in the midst of a seizure. Not only was she able to float upwards, but she could also float horizontally. When levitating, it seemed even her clothing was defying gravity, not falling down into the folds one would expect, possibly due to the rigidity of her body. Only sprinkling her with holy water could stop her levitation.

In addition, Clara had physical alterations; her cheeks would inflate beyond what seemed physically possible, her neck would lengthen causing a large goiter to appear, and lumps would appear under her skin and move across her body in front of witnesses. All of these manifestations would come and go and could not be rationally explained by those present.

Like many cases of demon possession, Clara was also able to both speak and understand languages she had never been taught including German, Polish, and French.

CLAIRVOYANCE

Clara also developed very disturbing clairvoyant abilities. One young man had viciously mocked her and her retaliation took the form of revealing numerous sins he had committed, including the date, time, and person with whom he committed them.

In another instance, she described in detail the recent journeys of one of the priests present. She knew specific destinations and times even hard for the priest to report, much less someone not travelling with him.

She could also read the impure thoughts of those around her, repeating them aloud and stating who was thinking them. It seemed absolutely nothing was hidden from the demons possessing Clara, nor were they reluctant to share what they knew. Needless to say, many of those who came into her presence quickly retreated.

STRANGE REACTIONS TO RELIGIOUS ITEMS

Clara knew if she or her food had been sprinkled with holy water and would bellow hysterically in a maniacal, hollow, mocking laugh.

Clara could also discern if a person in the room carried any type of religious relic, artifact, or even a crucifix, even if it was carefully hidden. This usually resulted in a very violent reaction on her part.

THE SNAKE

One of the most disturbing manifestations associated with Clara was her ability to undertake the movement and behavior of a snake.

Clara would suddenly fall to the floor, roll over onto her stomach, and place her arms tightly against her side. She would wriggle across the floor like a snake and witnesses said her movements seemed impossible for a normal human skeletal structure to accomplish. Others described it as rubbery, as if her bones had been replaced with some elastic substance.

Sometimes she would lay her throat flat on the floor while she slithered along, further emphasizing a snake-like appearance while other times she would flick her tongue out of her mouth.

In one incident, one of the nuns was kneeling on the floor praying for Clara's soul. Clara quickly wriggled over to her side, raised her head, and in serpentine-fashion darted her head forward towards the nun's arm and struck like a viper, biting deeply into the nun's arm. The other nuns quickly restrained Clara and the injured nun noticed that the bite mark resembled that a snake rather than a human.

THE EXORCISM

An exorcism was approved for Clara. As soon as the rite of exorcism started, she went into a trance-like state and was instantly on her feet, knocking the priest's Bible out of his hands and grabbing his stole. Before anyone had time to stop her, she pulled it tightly around his neck in an attempt to strangle him. Foul and blasphemous language poured forth from her as those present pulled her away from the priest. He continued on with the rite, unfazed and unimpressed.

The familial haunting bestial sounds filled the room as she began to levitate rigidly above the bed. Not until the priests present sprinkled her with holy water did she quickly fall back down.

Clara growled, snarled, and struggled desperately. Foul language and blasphemy poured from her as the rite continued. The last time she levitated, she fell back down without holy water being applied. Clara had been freed.

Not much detail is recorded about what happened during the exorcism itself, but it worked...for a while. It seems Clara made yet another pact with the Devil and the manifestations returned.

Another exorcism was performed and once again Clara was freed. Unlike the last time, however, a horrifically nauseating stench filled the room and then disappeared right before she was freed. Once freed, she asked for forgiveness for entering a pact with the Devil and apparently had no more problems. She died six years later of heart complications.

THIEBAULD & JOSEPH: THE POSSESSED BROTHERS

Thiebauld Burner was the eldest of five children in the Burner family in the year 1864. The Burner family was a hard working Catholic family of modest means with nothing out of the ordinary until the two oldest boys, Thiebauld and Joseph, suddenly fell ill. The boys, ages 9 and 7, developed bizarre symptoms that puzzled the local doctors.

SYMPTOMS BEGIN

Their symptoms were unusual, to say the least. The boys abdomens suddenly swelled to a grotesque size and they would complain it felt like a ball was rolling around in their stomachs or that some kind of animal was running loose in their body. This undoubtedly painful affliction baffled the doctors, who could neither find a cause nor a successful treatment.

The boys' language was suddenly filled with blasphemy and they spoke in unfamiliar languages most of their family did not understand. They became hostile towards priests and other religious leaders and refused to eat any food that had been sprinkled with holy water; contact with holy water made them squirm like a crushed worm.

Thiebauld, in particular, refused to go near a church. Even if he was blindfolded, he would begin to struggle and bay like a donkey if brought near a church or chapel.

They would go into inexplicable rages where they would attack the furniture as if they wanted to tear it to pieces and then suddenly go limp as if they had passed out. Anger, irregular behavior, and strange manifestations became the norm for them.

NIGHTTIME MANIFESTATIONS

At night, both boys would rapidly turn over from their back to their stomach and back again. As they would do this, they would hold their bodies rigid with their arms at their sides. This might not seem at unusual except the boys' parents claimed the turning occurred with such speed it seemed as if they were being spun by an unseen force.

Eventually, this disturbing turning was replaced by an even more physically inexplicable action. The boys would intertwine their legs and arms together, knotting themselves to each other. Onlookers described it as if the boys' arms and legs were made of rubber. Men, undoubtedly including their own father, attempted to disentangle them to pull them apart, but no amount of physical strength could unlock them.

CLAIRVOYANCE

Twice Thiebauld knew someone had died when it was not possible for him to know. In one instance it was an elderly woman and in another it was the father of a girl present. Thiebauld informed the girl her father was dead and she argued that he was in perfect health. Thiebauld countered, stating her father had taken a fatal fall. A few hours later, she learned her father had fallen to his death in a construction accident. It is worthy to note these statements from Thiebauld were accompanied by sadistic mockery and were spoken in a venomous fashion.

PHYSICAL IMPOSSIBILITIES

Records from the time indicate the boys could ascend trees with the speed and agility of a squirrel, using only their hands and feet. Once up a tree, they were able to perch on branches simply not strong enough to hold their weight.

After these symptoms started, these boys were also able to bend themselves in half, backwards and forward. They had never been flexible enough to do things like this before; it was simply unnatural.

PARANORMAL SIGNS

As is the case in many stories of possession, the boys could speak and understand English, French, German, Latin, and Spanish, as well as different dialects of these languages. While it is possible they may have heard some of these languages, they were considered poor students and were not known for studying, and making it doubtful they learned these languages by any natural means. In fact, Thiebauld's command of French while under possession was considered perfect.

Both boys also levitated, sometimes taking the furniture up in the air with them; objects in the room would randomly begin to fly around and windows would fly open on their own.

THE FEATHERED NIGHTMARE

Thiebauld was the only brother to see a creature, however. It was a large being covered in feathers with a bill like a duck and human hands that ended in terrible claws. When Thiebauld saw it, he would frantically fight it, screaming and crying that it was trying to strangle him. This would happen 20 to 30 times in a single day.

When it happened, a nauseating odor would fill the room and saturate his clothes causing his family no choice but to burn them. When they would remove Thiebauld's clothing, they would also find strange aquatic grass in them; there could provide no explanation for where it came from or how it ended up in his clothing.

EXORCISM

It took five long years of torment before the Catholic Church approved an exorcism for the boys. Thiebauld was first and his exorcism would take the longest.

A struggling, enraged, cursing Thiebauld was carried into the chapel strapped to a heavy chair carried by three men. He began to foam at the mouth profusely, twisting and turning his body as he looked for an exit.

Thiebauld kept insisting he didn't want to be exorcised, as blasphemy and hatred poured forth in a variety of languages. He bellowed the worst insults at the priest and fought the restraints with all his might as the priest began to pray. He screamed and howled as the rite of exorcism was administered. Shivering, trembling, and howling like a wolf –even snapping at the priest's hand like a wild, restrained animal, he struggled to the point the three men had great difficulty holding him down on the chair. After three hours, the priest was drenched with sweat and exhausted; he decided to continue the exorcism the following day.

On the second day of the exorcism, Thiebauld was placed in a straightjacket and again tied to the chair; however, as the chair was set down, it levitated in the air. After a considerable struggle, which included the large, strong men being inexplicably thrown with great force, they managed to get Thiebauld and the chair back down on the ground. Thiebauld again began to foam at the mouth so profusely that onlookers described it as jets of foam pouring forth from the corners of his mouth.

After about two hours, Thiebauld began to thrash about and a crash was heard. Suddenly, he lost consciousness and the demons were gone. Thiebauld awoke after about an hour with no recollection of what had happened during the exorcism or any memory of the past five years.

He was freed from demonic possession, but it seemed the torments he went through those five years as he waited for an exorcism took a toll on his body and he died only four years later at the age of 18.

His brother Joseph was next in line for an exorcism. While the demon inside of him boasted that it was much stronger than those inside of Thiebauld, his exorcism went much easier. It only took one man to restrain 12-year-old Joseph during the exorcism. He screamed and howled, pouring fourth ungodly language and insults. He made animalistic sounds, yapping like a dog one moment and squealing like a pig later on. However, unlike his brother, he was also calm part of the time.

Oddly, in Joseph's case, the demons kept requesting to be cast into animals such as a herd of swine or sheep. The priest leading the exorcism refused to allow this, ordering them back to Hell. As the demons were final cast out, Joseph puffed out his cheeks, his body exhibiting a terrible spasm, and he fell unconscious. Oddly enough, the rosary placed around his neck broke as the demon left.

Moments later his eyes opened and he stretched as if he had just awakened from a long nap. He had no memory of the exorcism and only isolated memories of the past five years.

Joseph lived another thirteen years, but the physical torments and aberrations experienced took a terrible toll on his physical systems.

Both boys were completely delivered from the demonic entities that possessed them, never to suffer those same torments and manifestations again. No theory was ever presented to explain how the boys came to be possessed.

BEWITCHED SOPHIA

A priest in 1920s Italy was shocked when a young, but very weary, woman told him a story that seemed unbelievable. Sophia was an attractive, married, mother of two children, suffering at the hands of demonic entities for seven long years. Before seeking the assistance of the priest, she had exhausted all other avenues of help; doctors declared a case of hysteria, but had no solution for her. The church was her last hope though she had not ruled out suicide out of desperation.

OUT OF CONTROL

Sophia was horrified when she first realized something was taking over her body against her will. She said she would dance until she literally dropped from absolute weariness, unable to stop until every last vestige of energy she had was completely spent.

Other times she would suddenly begin to act like an animal, leaping from chair to chair on all fours, barking, mewing, screaming, and roaring–wildly moving throughout the house like a trapped animal until her body finally gave way to exhaustion. Once these very active incidents ended, she would be swollen and bruised.

Her husband stated he would come home from work and hear the bestial sounds coming from inside the house, knowing something was wrong. Upon entering, he would find the house turned upside down and Sophia out of her mind leaping around the house like a wild animal. When she was in such a state, the children would either go outside to play or go to bed, happening so frequently it did not scare them anymore.

Sophia did other things she could not explain or had any interest in doing. People saw her sing operatic arias she had never heard and had no way of knowing. Additionally, she would mysteriously give what seemed to be lectures in a foreign language to a group that even she could not see.

VIOLENCE

Some of her manifestations hinted at latent violence. She would have an almost overwhelming urge to bite and tear at anything placed in her hands; at times, she would rush into a room pleading with her husband to hand her something. "I must tear something up! I've got to tear something up–spoil it–destroy it!" Nothing in the house was safe from the urges. By the time the exorcism took place, the family had very little left that Sophia hadn't destroyed.

If ever restrained, she would bite and scratch. Apparently, when under control of the demons, Sophia would exhibit extreme strength. Once her husband insulted one of the demons and Sophia grabbed hold of his throat with such ferocity and strength he barely escaped. Other times he would come in and find her hidden beneath one of the tables. Her entire body would be tensed up, like a beast ready to spring. Her shoulders would be hunched and her appearance was like that caught in a trap. If he called her name, a voice would reply, "I am Isabo and it is I who gives the orders!"

INCIDENTS IN CHURCH

After the problems started, she would go to mass and seek blessings from the priests. It would alleviate her symptoms for a short time, but no lasting help had been found. Much to her horror, one of the most dramatic manifestations she experienced occurred when she went to visit a parish priest in another area. She had been lent a horse and carriage and everything seemed to be going well until she got close the chapel; the horse refused to move one step further. Without even realizing what she was doing, Sophia hopped down from the carriage and ran two feet above the ground the remaining distance to the chapel, across a field and up a hill. Witnesses described it as flying; her feet did not touch the ground from the time she alighted from the carriage until she reached the chapel.

Animals in the area reacted violently to her approach that day with dogs barking frantically and chickens cackling maniacally as they ran for cover. As she arrived at the church, her feet returned to the ground and everyone in the church square ran in fear. Sophia entered the church, was blessed by the priest, and was much improved, but only for a little while.

EXORCISM

After several more incidents, it was decided something decidedly paranormal was going on and a group of priests, after careful study of her case and observation of her symptoms, concluded an exorcism was necessary.

Sophia was brought in for the exorcism and seated in a simple wooden chair. As the exorcism started, she stretched her body like a fierce feline awakening from a nap. As the Latin ritual began, Sophia suddenly leaned forward in the chair and leapt through the air with amazing agility, landing a considerable distance away. As she looked up, those present for the exorcism were taken aback.

Her face was barely recognizable, with witness describing it as taking on a "hideous aspect." She was holding herself differently, more like a beast than a woman. Her arms hung loosely at her sides as she stooped slightly forward with her knees slightly bent. A harsh, unfamiliar voice came from her lips, pouring out abuse and blasphemy toward the church, the Lord, and all present.

As the exorcism progressed, she suddenly broke free from those restraining her and attacked the priest. She grasped his robe in desperation while a horrific, tormented scream came forth from her. The priest sprinkled her with holy water and Sophia began to writher on the floor in pain and anguish. Onlookers said she behaved as if burning embers, rather than holy water, had been cast upon her.

Still fighting for her deliverance, the priest placed the corner of his stole on her shoulder. In the blink of an eye she was on her feet with amazing dexterity, rushing to escape and complaining about how terribly heavy the stole felt.

She began to vomit, but oddly enough it had no resemblance to food. As the demons began to weaken, screams of rage were replaced with wails of terror. Trembling and weakness took the place of the aggressive, bestial stances she had taken before. At the end of the first session, Sophia was utterly exhausted and remembered nothing of what had happened.

THE FINAL EXORCISM

In total, it took thirteen sessions for Sophia to be freed. At the final exorcism, her behavior was quite different. She sat quietly in the chair, her head sunk on her chest, her body limp in imminent defeat. As the exorcist began to speak, she slowly stood up, walked over to a mattress on the floor, and slowly stretched out upon it. To onlookers she resembled a corpse. The priest continued the rite. Sophia did not move a muscle, nor did a single sound come from her. This was completely at odds with her behavior at all of the previous exorcisms.

Still looking corpselike, she began to vomit. Her entire body was wracked with terrible spasms. Everyone present felt tremendous compassion for this poor woman struggling to keep her long, dark hair out of the abnormal vomit and barely strong enough to stay on her feet.

FREEDOM

Suddenly, Sophia stood up and pushed her hair back from her face, revealing gaunt cheeks, bloodshot eyes resting in cavernous hollows, and what seemed like a total limpness of all facial muscles. Her lower lip hung loose and her slender arms hung weakly at her sides. Whatever was manifesting itself through her carried the look of defeat and made Sophia unrecognizable to her loved ones.

Then, quietly, a voice spoke, "I am...going." Sophia's chin dropped to her chest as the priest continued to order the demons out. Then, another voice spoke; it was Sophia's voice, full of joy and hope. "I am cured!" she said quietly, looking all around. Departed was the strange look in her eyes and was replaced by her human face. Sophia had been set free.

Based on the demons rantings during the exorcism and some contents of what she vomited, it is believed Sophia was an unfortunate victim of witchcraft.

GISELLE: THE HOUSEWIFE AND THE HEALER

Giselle was a typical 1950s era British housewife with a two-year old daughter. Unfortunately, her entire life was turned upside after she sought help from a local "healer" with a less than spotless reputation.

HEALTH ISSUES

Giselle was tired, but that was to be expected of a harried mother of a toddler. Her fatigue seemed to be more unnatural, for along with it was weight-loss, dizziness, and extreme apathy. She had been to several doctors, and all the tests came back normal.

One doctor, however, decided what she needed was to spend three weeks in a place where she could get total rest. Still, their family's limited income prevented it and even if they had the money it was unlikely Giselle would be willing to go because she had never been away from her family for an extended time.

One day she was talking to a close friend who suggested she visit a "healer" named Mr. Smith. The friend insisted he had done so much good for her son after he was diagnosed with nerve problem. There was one thing that still puzzled her friend; Mr. Smith had cut a lock of her son's hair and held it between his fingers until a thin curl of blue smoke came from his hands. But Giselle's friend was sure Mr. Smith could help heal her woes.

Giselle decided to pay Mr. Smith a visit the next time he called on her friend's son. She confided this in her mother. Her mother was skeptical of Mr. Smith's powers and she advised Giselle against it. Giselle was desperate, however, and she and her husband met the healer.

HEALER SMITH

The interview with the healer began by asking for Giselle's full name and the month of her birth and then, as with the boy, Mr. Smith took a lock of Giselle's hair and held it between his thumb and forefinger. He held it tightly and closed his eyes as Giselle watched blue smoke curl up from his hand, but there was no smell of burning hair. When he opened his hand, the hair was gone.

His diagnosis was nerves and he said she would need two or three sessions with him to be cured. He then opened a flask set beside him; instead of drinking from it, he dipped his thumb in the liquid and watched the face of his watch on the opposite hand, carefully timing how long his thumb remained in the liquid. He then withdrew his thumb and grabbed Giselle's wrist. As he did so, his face turned bright red and his entire body tensed. He held her thumb this way for a few minutes.

Giselle fell asleep while he was holding her wrist. As he let go, she awakened. She later said she felt very confused, disoriented, and foggy. She also complained her head seemed to be heavier than it should be and was difficult to hold it up. Mr. Smith reassured her all was well and sent the couple on their way.

THE BEGINNING

That night at dinner, Giselle dropped her fork and her head crashed to the table. She fell sound asleep, awaking a short while later complaining everything just faded out right before she fell asleep. She tried to explain to her husband something was wrong, for this was not a normal sleep. She felt very dazed and worn out—and very, very hungry.

At bedtime, she began to stare at the ceiling, seeing something her husband could not see. Next, she recited strange words her husband didn't recognize and started jabbering incoherently and would periodically let out a mocking laugh or a derisive snicker. Her movements were erratic and senseless as she circled the room, pointing at random objects. When her husband tried to restrain her, Giselle violently shoved him away.

A SECOND VISIT

They paid another visit to the healer to get help for these queer symptoms. Mr. Smith blamed it on her birth month and said he should have been more careful. In his experience, people born in Giselle's birth month were much more sensitive to the treatment.

Giselle fell asleep while they were talking. Mr. Smith reassured them that all was well; Giselle should simply go home and get a good night's sleep.

They went home and, as predicted, Giselle ate, consuming an entire bunch of bananas in one setting. She then fell into a very, very deep sleep. The next morning, she awoke suffering from confusion and feeling like she was walking in a haze.

MORE SYMPTOMS

She also began to develop severe headaches, though never had trouble with headaches before. Other times a terrible pain would come over her and leave her in tears.

Rather than recovering from the fatigue and weariness she had sought the healer for, things were becoming much, much worse. She was distraught and haggard, spending more and more of her time staring at the ceiling with her eyes wide open and fixed.

She would randomly fall asleep during the day for about an hour and half. Her husband described it as the sleep of the dead in which she wouldn't respond to any type of stimulation. Her family found it downright frightening.

Soon Giselle began to struggle with terribly strong urges to strangle her two-year-old daughter. She resisted with all her might and once the urge was gone, she would break down into tears, horrified the thought had even entered her mind, much less that she actually had to fight the urge. She began to feel it was best for her daughter's safety not to be home until this nightmare was over.

A THIRD VISIT

They visited the healer again and Mr. Smith gave her a tonic that supposedly contained ox blood and hemoglobin with added crystals to make it easier on her sensitive system. He also indicated if he was going to work with her she needed to be closer to him, suggesting a local hotel.

A few days after she was checked in, Giselle was no better. Much of the time she didn't recognize her own husband and wanted him to leave. She grew weaker and weaker under Mr. Smith's supposed treatment and soon was not able to eat or sleep. Her husband brought her home, overwhelmed and hopeless.

The doctors had not been able to help her; psychologists tried and found nothing wrong, but Giselle was terrified that she was descending into madness. They tried another healer, but it only seemed to help for a short while.

LEGAL ISSUES AND CONSEQUENCES

Eventually, they pressed legal charges against Mr. Smith. This led to more problems and he threatened to send Giselle into insanity if they didn't drop the charges. They did so, but the courts pursued a case based on the charge of practicing medicine without a license.

This led to a new and terrifying aspect of Giselle's living nightmare. She began to see visions of a horrible reptilian creature with a scaled body, legs that ended in enormous claws, and the face of Mr. Smith. She would scream and scream for help, hours on end, but no one could help her.

Eventually, a sort of delirium set in. She began speaking in foreign languages, moving erratically, and shrieking a hideous laugh not her own. When she would come back to herself, she would remember nothing. Then it would all start over when she saw the creature again.

EXORCISM

Her family suspected demonic possession when they saw how she began to react to crosses, rosaries, and holy water. They turned to the church and met with a sympathetic priest. Her symptoms began to improve and they discovered he had been performing minor exorcisms from a distance. They converted to Catholicism and began attending mass, which was difficult for Giselle, but she persisted.

Once the church had approved an exorcism, they met with the priest who would perform the exorcism. To her husband's horror, she leaped in the air and began to dance on her toes, flying around the room frantically when she met the priest.

As the ritual began, she was restrained. Blasphemy, filth, and insults began to pour from her. When not restrained, she would fall to the floor and begin to claw desperately at the floor, tearing it up with her fingers and fingernails, but seemingly oblivious to the pain.

When those assisting would try to pick her up, she weighed an estimated three times her normal body weight. The only way to move her was to drag her and it was excessively difficult to even hold on to her. This process went on for a total of fifteen months. The exorcist discovered the healer had placed a curse on her with the intent of making her his mistress. When she didn't respond to him the way he expected, he used dark forces to try to drive her insane. He failed.

She was freed of the demon and the curse and went on to live a completely normal life.

SLEEP WELL

You have just read multiple true stories of demon possession. One thing is sure: the dark powers portrayed in these stories are not our friends. They take pleasure in tormenting both the minds and bodies of those they possess. From trying to convince their victims to murder those they love the most to horribly twisting them in physical contortions the human body could not endure, these demons enjoyed their diabolical work.

To try to contact a demon or interact with one for entertainment, thrill seeking, or some type of benefit is beyond dangerous—it is surely destructive. Violence, murder, chaos, rage, and blasphemy follow in their wake and it takes a special type of person to challenge their claim to a human body.

Remember, demon possession is not the same as mental or physical illness. There is some overlap between the symptoms of certain metal disorders and the generally acknowledged signs of possession, such as hearing voices or experiencing bouts of extreme anger. Convulsions can be considered a symptom of demon possession, but they are also a symptom of a whole host of medical disorders.

In short, just because someone exhibits the symptoms of demon possession doesn't mean they are indeed possessed. A mistake can cost someone his or her life, as believed to be the case in the exorcism of Anneliese Michel.

Anneliese, a young, Catholic, German college student, heard voices, developed a dislike for religious objects, became aggressive, and practiced self-harm, among other symptoms. She became convinced she was possessed and died a terrible death at the hands of a misguided exorcism team. Her parents and the two main priests involved in administering the rite of exorcism were found guilty of homicide by the German government.

Experts looking back on the case today believe it was likely a combination of epilepsy, side effects of prescriptions for psychosis, and mental illness. Sadly, they believe Anneliese could have been treated with medication and lived a normal life. Instead, she died at the age of 24, weighing a mere 68 pounds, her body wasted away from near starvation and her knees fractured and too weak to move.

The possibility of illness, either mental or physical, should always be eliminated before an exorcism is performed. A responsible exorcist will leave no stone unturned in seeking out the root cause of the problem. If the cause is found to be diabolical in nature, a responsible exorcist will then fight to see the afflicted completely delivered.

In conclusion, the powers of darkness are very real and are not to be taken lightly. Be careful what you dabble in, or you might end up like one of the people you just read about.

DID YOU ENJOY *REAL DEMONIC POSSESSIONS AND EXORCISMS?*

Again let me thank you for purchasing and reading this short collection of stories. There are a number of great books out there, so I really appreciate you choosing this one.

If you enjoyed the book, I'd like to ask for a small favor in return. If possible, I'd love for you to take a couple of minutes to leave a review for this book on Amazon. Your feedback will help me to make improvements to this book, as well as writing books on other topics that might be of interest to you!

OTHER BOOKS BY ZACHERY KNOWLES

Real Haunted Ouija Boards

Real Haunted Cemeteries and Graveyards

Real Demonic Possessions and Exorcisms

Real Haunted Woods and Forests

Real Police Ghost Stories

Real Haunted Castles and Fortresses

Real Haunted Hospitals and Mental Asylums

Real Hauntings at Sea

FREE GIFT REMINDER

Before you finish, I'd like to remind you one more time of the free eBook I'm offering to readers of my *True Ghost Stories* series.

To instantly download the PDF version of my book, *Real Black-Eyed Kids*, all you need to do is visit:

<u>www.realhorror.net</u>

Printed in Great Britain
by Amazon